David's Secret Soccer Goals

David's Secret Soccer Goals

Caroline Levine

Jessica Kingsley Publishers
London and Philadelphia

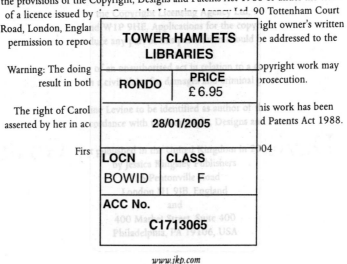

First published in the United Kingdom in 2004
by Jessica Kingsley Publishers
116 Pentonville Road
London N1 9JB, England

and

400 Market Street, Suite 400
Philadelphia, PA 19106, USA

www.jkp.com

Copyright © Caroline Levine 2004

Library of Congress Cataloging in Publication Data
Levine, Caroline Anne.
    David's secret soccer goals / Caroline Levine.
        p. cm.
    Summary: David wants to go to soccer camp, but first he must try to solve his bed-wetting problem.
    ISBN 1-84310-772-4 (pbk.)
    [1. Bedwetting--Fiction. 2. Soccer--Fiction. 3. Family life--Fiction.] I. Title.
    PZ7.L57832Dav 2004
    [Fic]--dc22
                                                    2003026440

British Library Cataloguing in Publication Data
A CIP catalogue record for this book is available from the British Library

ISBN 1 84310 772 4

Printed and Bound in Great Britain by
Athenaeum Press, Gateshead, Tyne and Wear

Many thanks to the following people who've given me insight into the problems of children who bed-wet and some of the solutions that work for them:

Stanley Hellerstein, MD
Rod Levine, MD
Ann Hellerstein, MD
Joseph Lopreiato, MD
Cindy Straub, RN.

Contents

Chapter One

Good News/Bad News

"**Y**our socks look like Christmas!" my sister, Jayne the Pain, told me. Mom was driving me to soccer practice after school. Jayne was in the back with me.

I looked at my socks. So one had green stripes at the top and the other red ones—big deal. I had wet the bed last night and had to take a shower before school. I wanted to say she had cereal stuck in her braces, but I said, "Got dressed fast." No sense asking for trouble.

"Why's that?" she asked. "Had to take a shower?"

"Jayne!" Mom said in her warning voice. "I don't like where this is going."

When I was getting out of the car, I overheard Mom say, "You know, Jayne, he's not the only one with a night problem."

Night problem? Did Jayne wet, too? If she did, she sure was good at hiding it!

"Hey," Matt said, running up to me, "I've got a new riddle."

"What?" I said, blinking. I didn't see him coming because I was concentrating on Jayne.

"Why did the coach send a sub into the gym?" he asked.

"Because he had to leave school?" I guessed.

"No," Matt said, "because the gym was flooded. You know, sub, substitute?"

"Funny," I said, running onto the soccer field. Matt caught up with me. We found a soccer ball and started dribbling.

Then I stopped and tried the instep kick. The dumb ball flew the other way. "I'll never learn that kick!" I told him.

"Uh huh," he said, "look how good you dribble."

"Okay, Hawks," Coach yelled, "front and center."

Matt and I sat in the cold grass and gently kicked the ball back and forth. Coach doesn't mind this as long as we listen.

"Kids, today we're going to work some more on the instep kick."

Everyone groaned, me the loudest.

Coach held up his hand. "Look," he said, "I know it's hard, but it's an important kick to master. Learn this, and you can make the ball go exactly where you want."

That would be very useful, I thought, but the bicycle kick is cooler. I pictured myself jumping high in the air and blasting the ball with my powerful kick.

Coach held up one foot and rubbed his shoelaces. "Remember," he said, "this is the part that hits the ball for the instep kick." He dumped a bag of balls on the grass. "Grab a partner and practice those insteps."

"On the shoelaces," I whispered to myself as I kicked the ball. But it kept going all over the place. After about two thousand tries, I kicked the ball straight to Matt.

"You did it!" he shouted. He's never jealous when something good happens to me.

"So will you," I answered. "We'll just keep practicing." Matt gave me the thumbs-up sign.

Coach ran over to me. "David, with kicking like that, you're going to love my surprise."

"What surprise?" Matt and I said. Coach's last surprise was new jerseys with scary hawks on the back.

Coach blew his whistle and the rest of the team ran over. He took a fat envelope from his pocket. "You kids are getting good," he told us. "So I think you're going to love soccer camp."

That was the good news. "Yes!" everyone cried. Matt and I gave each other a high five.

Coach opened the envelope and passed out colored brochures. "I'll be going," he said, "I've signed up for the coach camp."

"Look!" I told Matt when I opened my brochure. There were pictures of kids playing in teams, kids watching a soccer movie, and kids heading balls in a big pool.

"Cool!" Matt said, pointing to another picture.

That was the bad news. My stomach felt like it had just caught a zooming ball. The picture was of guys in a cabin—in *sleeping bags*! Sleep-away camp. No way could I go.

"Team," Coach explained above the noise, "we get a discount if we send in our money by April tenth. That's three months from now. Ask your folks about it tonight."

I was glad when it was time to go. I jammed the brochure into my shorts and ran down to the car.

Chapter Two

Trouble With The Brochure

Jayne, the Pain, was in the back seat. I wished Pelé, my cat, was there instead.

"Why's your pocket so fat?" she asked. "Your diaper."

"Stop that right now!" Mom told her. "They're disposable underpants, and you know darn well he only wears them at night."

"It's just a stupid brochure," I told Jayne.

Mom glanced at me in the rearview mirror. "David," she said, "you looked upset after practice. Something about that brochure."

"Yeah," I said, drumming my fingers on the armrest. "Tell you later."

I felt something funny. I looked down and saw Jayne sneaking the brochure out of my shorts. She'd make a great pickpocket.

"Give it back!" I yelled. I reached for it, but she waved it around too fast.

"Champions' soccer camp," she read in her microphone voice, "where boys and girls play soccer 24/7 and where David Roberts pees in his…"

"Jayne!" Mom yelled, pulling the car over. "That is so mean! Apologize."

"I'm sorry," she said in a fake way.

When we got home, Jayne took the last bag of chips and went to her room. I found a jar of cheese and some crackers for Mom and me.

"So, do you want to go to this camp?" Mom asked. She was looking right into my eyes.

"Sort of," I mumbled, "sort of not."

"Is it about your night problem?"

"Yeah," I said, spreading cheese on lots of crackers. I slid the plate over to Mom. I wasn't hungry anymore.

Mom read the brochure. "We'll have to talk this over with Dad."

"Why?" I asked. "He'll say kids who wet don't deserve to go to camp."

Mom shut her eyes for a few seconds. "We don't know that for sure," she told me. "We have to ask anyway."

Mom didn't say anything more, but I guess she knew how crummy I felt because she made my favorite dinner, hamburger and fries.

After dinner, I loaded the dishwasher and changed Pelé's water. As I was leaving, Jayne started to wipe the counters. I hoped she'd finish soon and go yack on the phone.

Mom and Dad were in the family room waiting for me. I took my little soccer ball from the shelf and passed it between my feet. Mom always bragged to people that I kicked it around my playpen when I was only six months old.

I looked up and saw Jayne watching through the crack in the door. Dad saw her too. "I can't believe you'd be so sneaky," he yelled. "Go to your room."

Of course, I already knew she was sneaky, but I didn't know if she wet the bed.

I was glad when I heard Jayne's door slam, but I wished I was upstairs too. I hated talking about my problem.

Chapter Three

Not The Only One

Dad tapped my brochure on his knee. "Looks like a great camp," he said.

"Yeah," I said, concentrating on my ball. That way, when Dad started in again about my wetting, maybe it wouldn't hurt so much.

"But kids who wear diapers at night would have a problem there," he said, still tapping away.

"Brad!" Mom yelled. "They aren't called diapers. Can't you be a little more tactful."

Tactful, like full of tacks? That's exactly how he sounded.

"Call them whatever you want, Nancy," Dad shot back. "All I know is they're expensive and he should stop that wetting."

A rotten feeling washed over me. What was wrong with me? Why did I wet? No one else did.

"Is that what you did, Brad," Mom screamed at Dad, "just tell yourself to stop one night?" She snapped her fingers at him. "Stopped, just like that, huh?"

My mouth hung open. I couldn't believe Dad used to wet the bed.

Dad glared at Mom and jumped out of his chair. "You didn't have to tell him!" he roared, stomping out of the room.

I started to cry. Mom rocked me like I was a little kid. I liked her on my side, but I felt dumb. And what if Jayne came down and saw me?

Mom fished a tissue out of her sleeve and blew her nose. "Honey," she said, "I shouldn't have said anything about Dad wetting. I embarrassed him."

"I don't get it," I yelled. "If Dad used to wet, why doesn't he understand? I hate wetting! Doesn't he know I'd stop if I could?" I started to cry harder because nothing made sense.

Mom held me tighter. "He loves you, and it hurts him to see you down, especially over something that used to make him miserable, too."

If he loves me, I thought, he sure has a funny way of showing it.

Mom got up and pushed my soccer ball with her toe, her ballerina kick. "Honey," she said, rolling it to me, "I think you should see Dr. Frankel. Maybe he can help."

"No way!" I said, leaving. "He'll think I'm a baby."

"Uh..." Mom said quietly, "your cousin Heather's doctor didn't think she was a baby."

I spun around so fast I got dizzy. "Heather wets the bed? But she's a goalie!" She was thirteen, Jayne's age, and was a goalie on a traveling ice-hockey team. I couldn't believe it.

"She *used* to wet," Mom said, studying a freckle on her arm. "It runs in Dad's family because Dad, Uncle Roger and Auntie Paula all wet, and it seems it got passed down to you and Heather. Aunt Tammy told me once that Heather was having trouble with sleep-overs, so they took her to the doctor. She was around eight, then."

Did this mean Mom told Aunt Tammy about me? I didn't ask.

Mom gave me a hug. "Tell you what, David," she said, "think about it."

My eye caught the brochure on the floor. A kid in one of the pictures was about to kick a ball in my direction. His eyes seemed to be looking at me, daring me to stop that ball.

I went to my room, to think. After all, Coach was always telling us to use our noggins for more than heading.

Later, I told Mom it was okay to call Dr. Frankel.

Chapter Four

More Good News/Bad News

After school the next day, Matt and I played in his backyard. We dribbled for a while, then took turns doing the instep kick.

I blasted the ball to the end of the yard.

Matt said, "Wait til the kids at camp see you."

"Uh huh," I said, shrugging. I pivoted and air kicked the other way so he wouldn't see my face. I'm not good at hiding stuff.

"You sound like you don't want to go," Matt said. He rolled another ball to me.

I kicked it back. "Oh I do," I lied, "it's just that I have to visit my great-grandpa Roberts. I'm going the day camp starts." I didn't know I could lie that fast. I wasn't proud of it.

Matt looked at me funny. "I didn't know you had a great-grandpa."

"Yeah," I said, heading the ball to him. "He's very old."

Matt put his foot on top of the ball. "But it won't be any fun if you don't go."

I looked at the sky. "I have to go—he's one hundred and three and he could be in Heaven soon."

My heart started to pound. What if I decided to go to camp? What would I say about not seeing Great-Grandpa Roberts? If I said he got better and Matt, Mr. Polite, told Mom he was glad to hear it, I'd be grounded for life. The thing is, I couldn't say Great-Grandpa Roberts got better since he's dead.

When I got home, Mom told me we were going to Dr. Frankel's tomorrow, after soccer practice.

"Oh," was all I said. The good news was, it would be over by this time tomorrow. The bad news was, it was going to be embarrassing.

Chapter Five

A Jumpy Day

I was nervous all day—from the time I woke up wet til Mom picked me up at the park.

"How was practice?" she asked.

"Just a second," I said. My hands were shaking so much, I couldn't get my seatbelt to click. "Coach said my instep kicks are getting good." I didn't tell her I'd flubbed about a hundred of them because I was so jumpy.

I snapped my wristband all the way to the doctor's.

Dr. Frankel's nurse put Mom and me in a little room. "What's the doctor seeing you for?" she asked me.

I felt my face burn. "Wetting at night," I whispered. I hoped she wouldn't have to repeat the question.

The nurse opened a cabinet and took out a little plastic cup with a lid. "Then Dr. Frankel will want a urine sample," she said. She wrote my name on the cup, gave it to me and pointed to the bathroom. "Pee in this and when you're done, leave it on the counter. Then wait for the doctor on the examining table."

I locked the bathroom door and took the lid off the cup. I was so nervous I could've filled a bucket, but I filled the cup and peed the rest in the toilet.

I'd just hopped onto the examining table when Dr. Frankel knocked on the door.

"Come in," Mom said.

"Good to see you, David," Dr. Frankel said, shaking my hand. Then he opened my chart. "Wetting at night..." he read out loud. He looked up at me. "I bet you think you're the only one who does this."

I nodded.

"I see kids with this problem, including girls, almost every single week. In fact, in your class, there are probably at least two or three other kids who wet the bed."

I grinned. It felt so good to know I wasn't the only one. Only I wished I knew who they were.

Dr. Frankel went to the counter and poured a little of my pee on a microscope slide.

"David," he asked, "are you wetting more often? Do you pee more during the day? Does it hurt to pee?"

I watched him fit the slide onto his microscope and lower his head to it. "No, to all three," I answered. "It's just that I want to go to camp, soccer camp, and I want to quit wetting."

"I see," Dr. Frankel said. "Good news here— you don't have an infection. I'll examine you, ask some questions, then we'll go over your options."

Options—I'd never heard of them. Were they part of my body? I looked over at Mom.

"Options are choices," she told me, smiling.

Dr. Frankel listened to my heart and lungs, tapped a little rubber hammer on my knees, then poked around my belly. "You have a fine healthy boy here," he told Mom.

"I thought so," she said, "but then why's he stuck with this problem? Because his father had it too?"

Dr. Frankel told me to sit up. "Bed-wetting often runs in families," he explained to Mom and me. Then he pointed to a big chart of someone's insides. "Here's what a full bladder looks like. It could be that David has a small one for now, but it will grow and hold more urine as he gets older."

To me, it looked like a pink balloon with an extra long stem.

"Or, maybe he's such a sound sleeper that he doesn't wake up when he needs to," he added. "Sometimes kids have to learn to make the brain and bladder cooperate better."

"David," Dr. Frankel asked me, "when you started playing soccer, how long before your feet obeyed your brain."

I blew out a long breath. "For the instep kick," I said, "forever."

"There are things you can use to help train your brain and bladder: medications, moisture alarms, charts, rewards and washing machines."

"Washing machines?" Mom blurted out.

Dr. Frankel winked at me. "We don't know why it works, but often when bed wetters help wash their sheets or pajamas, things get better. I said 'help,' not do the whole thing. It should *never* be used as a punishment."

He walked over to a cabinet, opened a drawer and took out a box. "Here are your options," he told me.

There were a bottle of pills, some kind of nose spray, disposable underpants, a pad with a cloth cover going to a control box, a comic book, a candy bar, a chart, and a little booklet. "If it's all right with you two," he said, "I'd like to try the pad, chart and rewards first. For many kids, that's all they need."

"How long will it take for this pad to help me?" I asked.

Dr. Frankel put his hand on my shoulder. "Anywhere between a few weeks and a few months," he answered. "You'll probably have accidents for a while, everyone does."

"It's important that the whole family supports David on this," he told Mom. "That means no teasing, no belittling, no blaming."

Mom and I looked at each other. I think we were both thinking, *"Tell that to Jayne and Dad!"*

"And remember, if at some point, you want to try medication, that's all right, too."

I put my hand in my pocket and counted silently on my fingers: February, March, April—enough time for the pad to work. If it did, I'd sign up for camp.

"I'll try that pad thing," I told Mom.

Dr. Frankel said we could buy the pad kit at a drugstore or online. He told me to call if there were problems, or to share good progress. He shook my hand again and said, "David, training your brain and bladder to work together isn't easy. It's going to take a while, but I know you can do it."

Chapter Six

Setting Up The Alarm

Mom and I went to the drugstore and bought a moisture alarm kit, comic books, trading cards and all different kinds of candy bars.

When we got home, I heard Jayne blabbing on the phone upstairs. Good—that meant she wouldn't see what we'd bought.

Mom and I went to my room to set up the alarm kit. It came with a chart, some stickers that said *I got up at night!* and a training booklet. I tacked the chart above my desk.

Mom read the booklet to me. I was to date a square each morning and then mark whether I woke up wet or dry. I was to add a sticker if I woke up and peed in the bathroom at night. I was feeling good about the kit until Jayne came banging down the stairs and into my room.

"What's that?" she asked, pointing to the alarm pad on my bed.

"None of your beeswax!" I said, grabbing my pillow and throwing it over the pad.

"Let me see!" she said, sweeping aside the pillow. "A heating pad? What a good idea. Now you won't have to lie in your cold pee."

"Stop it, Jayne!" Mom yelled. "For your information, it's a moisture pad to help your brother get to soccer camp."

I hated my problem! I went to the kitchen to have a soda. When I heard Jayne walking off to her room, I went back with it.

Mom looked up. "We're going to have a family meeting tonight," she said. "Jayne has got to stop this teasing, and Dad needs to know how courageous you are."

"I am?" I asked, putting the soda on my nightstand.

"Yes," she said, ruffling my hair. "It took a lot of courage to see Dr. Frankel, and now you have the courage to tackle your problem."

After dinner we all sat around the table. Mom explained that we'd bought the alarm kit and rewards and how they were supposed to work together.

"Mom," Jayne yelled, "he gets rewards for not wetting? It's not fair! I don't wet and what do I get? Absolutely nothing."

Bam! Dad hit the table with his fist. "Jayne," he shouted, "if you needed rewards to get rid of a problem, you'd get them, too."

"What about my th..." Jayne began. She clapped her hand over her mouth and tore out of the room.

Aha, I thought, so her problem starts with "th." Did she have a problem with thinking? But why would it be just at night?

Mom and Dad were talking about how to stop Jayne's teasing when something started buzzing.

"What's that?" we asked, looking around.

A second later, Pelé charged into the kitchen, his fur standing straight up. He jumped on top of the refrigerator, his safe place. We followed the noise to my room.

"It's my moisture alarm," I said. I pointed to the big wet spot on the pad. Pelé had knocked over my soda and it'd splashed on the pad. When we stopped laughing, Mom showed me how to turn off the alarm.

"This thing's clever!" Dad said. He sat on my bed and picked up the pad and control. "So, it'll buzz and wake you up?" he asked me.

"Should," I said. Then I heard Jayne running into my room. "Only Pelé doesn't need it," she said, "because he uses the litter box. Otherwise, he'd wear P-a-m-p-u-r-r-s, she spelled. Get it? Pampers—diapers for cats."

"Jayne!" Dad hollered, "This teasing is going to stop right now, understand? Teasing only makes the problem worse."

I felt better when I saw Mom flash Dad a big smile. Jayne made her eyes into slits at me, then left in a huff.

Mom, Dad and I discussed the awards. The trading cards, comics and candy bars would be for making small goals, like staying dry for two nights or getting up at night to use the bathroom. There would be a bigger surprise for two weeks of dry nights. Whoa, I thought, will I ever have two weeks of dry nights?

Chapter Seven

A Hard Goal

The next morning, I woke up in a cold puddle. I reached over to pet Pelé but he'd taken off. I socked my pillow, got up and checked the "wet" box on my chart. Then I remembered that Dr. Frankel told me I'd sleep through the alarm at first.

I yanked the sheets off, put them in the washer and took a shower.

At breakfast, Jayne had a nasty look on her face. She started to say something to me, then stopped. Maybe she knew she'd be grounded if Mom or Dad caught her teasing me.

Five nights later, I was having an odd dream—the fire alarm was buzzing at school. It was weird, because even in my dream I knew the sound was different than the real one. When I woke up, I saw Pelé bolting off the bed and knew

I had to pee. I ran to the bathroom and finished. "Yes!" I said, punching the air. I'd get to mark the "dry" box and put the special sticker on the chart in the morning.

On the way back to bed, I noticed Jayne's door open a crack. I looked in. "No way!" I whispered. "A night-light!" I tiptoed over to get a better look. It was the top of an old-fashioned streetlamp, kind of cool. I'd never seen it before, so I guessed she plugged it in at night after I went to bed.

On my way out, I saw something even more surprising. Jayne was sucking her thumb! So that was her "th" problem. Was it a problem because it would wreck her braces? Make her teeth stick out again?

On my eighth chart day, I told Mom I had had another dry night. Jayne heard and saw Mom give me a candy bar for my lunch.

"Good job," Jayne told me. She sounded like she meant it, so I gave her a piece. But why was she being nice to me?

The next Saturday I woke up wet—I'd slept through the alarm. I pulled off my sheets and dumped them in the washer. I thought I'd save Mom some work, so I put in some soap and pressed the start button. Back in my room I smelled something soapy. It seemed to be coming from the laundry room, so I checked it out.

Yikes! The floor was covered with bubbles. I ran to my parents' room. "Mom," I cried, "what do you do when the washer's barfing?"

Mom stopped making the bed. "Is this a riddle?" she asked.

"No," I said, taking Mom's hand. We raced to the laundry room.

Mom looked at the sudsy floor. "Well, the answer is, Mom teaches you how to use a mop and bucket. Then you get a lesson on how to run the washer."

I had to learn fast because I had a soccer game in half an hour. We beat the Rockets 2–1. When it was over, Coach came up to me and Matt as we were loading the ball bag. "David," he told me, "that was fine kicking on your assist. Just think what you'll do after camp."

"But Coach," Matt said, "he can't go."

Coach frowned. "Is there a problem, David?"

I looked away. "I have to visit my great-grandfather when camp starts," I lied. My stomach lurched.

Coach hoisted the bag of balls over his shoulder. "See if you can change the date," he told me.

I gulped. "I'll try," I said, wiping the sweat off my forehead. I wished I'd never started this stupid lie.

Soon it was time to decide about camp. I counted twelve "dry" marks on my chart. I stared at it, wishing it could tell me if I should sign up or not. I flopped down on my bed and thought about my options. I could ask for medications. I could take my night pants. No! I thought, the guys will find out. But they work when you sleep over at Matt's, a little voice said inside my head. I went back and forth like that for a long time. I read the camp pamphlet again and studied every picture. The ones of kids heading in the pool and telling jokes in the cabin did it—I decided to sign up.

Ten days later, I showed Mom the fifteen "dry" marks on my chart. She gave me a new wristband.

"Super," I said, slipping it on, "it's the Hawks' colors."

Mom smirked at me. "I don't go to all those games for nothing."

Then I caught a bad cold, and for a week I had more wet nights than dry ones. Mom called Dr. Frankel. He said that happens sometimes when kids get sick, and that I'd be dry again in a few days.

Six weeks before camp, I counted my dry nights. I took Dad into my room and I showed him the chart—I'd been mostly dry for seven weeks.

"Wait here," he told me. He came back hiding something behind his back. "You've worked hard for this, David. Here's something to help you celebrate." He tossed a fat sack to me.

The sack was taped shut, but I ripped it open in two seconds. It was a brand new sleeping bag! I wrapped my arms around it, feeling how soft and puffy it was. "Thanks, Dad!" I said. I felt like I'd just made the winning goal in a playoff game, with Dad cheering like crazy.

Chapter Eight

Night Before Camp

The night before camp, Mom and I were packing my duffel bag. I made an anti-wet kit with night pants, wipes and little plastic sacks. I'd keep the kit in my sleeping bag. If I woke up wet, I'd slip off the pants inside my bag, roll them up tight and put them in the sack. Then I'd hide it up my pajama sleeve, go outside and throw it in the trash.

Sure about this? I asked myself. I took the kit out of my duffel bag. Then I put it back in. I took it out again.

"Should I take my wet kit?" I asked Mom.

"Hmm," she said, pointing to my chart. "Well, you've been mostly dry."

"But that's *here*," I explained. "What if it's spooky at night and I'm afraid to go to the latrine? What if my brain and bladder get tired and don't wake me up? Don't forget, I won't have my moisture alarm." I put the kit back in.

Mom smiled and said, "You always did plan ahead."

After Mom left, Jayne came in. She had a nice look on her face, but her hand was plastered against her pocket. Was she hiding some kind of practical joke like a hand buzzer or squirting water pen? I liked those things, but not on me.

"David," she said, "it's going to be dark and scary at night when you're in your sleeping bag."

I stared at her mysterious pocket. "Uh huh," I answered.

"And *I* know that *you* know about my problem."

I ran into my closet and slammed the door. This was bad. I held the doorknob tight against me. She knocked softly. "I'm not going to do anything," she said. "You can come out."

I opened the door a crack and took a fast peek. She was holding up both hands to show she wasn't going to hurt me. I stepped out carefully.

"When you snooped around my room that night, I was just pretending to be asleep. I saw you looking at my night-light and then my thumb."

I held my breath.

"When you leaned over me, I wanted to punch you, hard. I didn't because you would've screamed and woken up Mom and Dad—then we'd both be in big trouble."

I rolled my eyes as I pictured them scared, then mad.

Jayne patted her pocket. "Well," she said, "thanks for not saying anything about…my problem. It's so embarrassing."

I wondered if she meant using the night-light or sucking her thumb?

She reached in her pocket. "Anyway, I have something for you." She pulled out a skinny red flashlight and tossed it to me. "It's for getting up in the middle of the night when you have to go, so you won't be scared to walk to the latrine."

"Thanks, Jayne!" I said, turning it on. It had a strong beam. "It'll be perfect."

I didn't say I'd packed my wet kit. So what if I did?